DECKY DOES A BRONCO

T0262476

Douglas Maxwell

DECKY DOES A BRONCO

OBERON BOOKS
LONDON

WWW.OBERONBOOKS.COM

First published in 2001 by Oberon Books Ltd
521 Caledonian Road, London N7 9RH
Tel: +44 (0) 20 7607 3637 / Fax: +44 (0) 20 7607 3629
e-mail: info@oberonbooks.com
www.oberonbooks.com

Copyright © Douglas Maxwell 2001

Douglas Maxwell is hereby identified as author of this play in
accordance with section 77 of the Copyright, Designs and Patents
Act 1988. The author has asserted his moral rights.

All rights whatsoever in this play are strictly reserved and
application for performance etc. should be made before
commencement of rehearsal to United Agents, 12-26 Lexington
Street, London W1F 0LE (info@unitedagents.co.uk). No
performance may be given unless a licence has been obtained,
and no alterations may be made in the title or the text of the play
without the author's prior written consent.

This book is sold subject to the condition that it shall not by way
of trade or otherwise be circulated without the publisher's consent
in any form of binding or cover or circulated electronically other
than that in which it is published and without a similar condition
including this condition being imposed on any subsequent
purchaser.

A catalogue record for this book is available from the British
Library.

PB ISBN: 978-1-84002-243-8
E ISBN: 978-1-84943-816-2

Cover image by Douglas Jones

Visit www.oberonbooks.com to read more about all our books
and to buy them. You will also find features, author interviews and
news of any author events, and you can sign up for e-newsletters
so that you're always first to hear about our new releases.

For Mum, Dad and Mazza
And for Colin, who gave me the idea
and was nothing like Barry.

Contents

Side-on View of a Bronco

1. Get a good speed up...

2. Put a foot behind the swing...

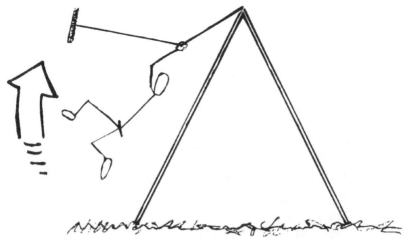

3. Pull chains, lean back and kick swing over you...

4. Keep moving forward! Swing goes over the bar.

Decky Does A Bronco was first performed at Brodie Park, Paisley on 28 July 2000, before embarking on a Scottish tour, with the following cast:

DECKY, David Ireland
DAVID, Keith Macpherson
YOUNG CHRISSY, Andy Clark
ADULT CHRISSY, Craig Smith
YOUNG BARRY, Ross Sutherland
ADULT BARRY, Paul Cunningham
YOUNG O'NEIL, Jimmy Harrison
ADULT O'NEIL, Muz Murray

Producer, Judith Doherty
Director, Ben Harrison
Sculptor/Set Designer, Allan Ross
Costume Designer, Alice Bee
Lighting Designer, George Tarbuck
Composer, Philip Pinsky
Stunt Co-ordinator, Jonothan Campbell
Company Stage Manager, Amy Shapcott
Deputy Stage Manager, Ross McDade
Production Assistants, Deborah Crewe, Sunita Hinduja

The play was revived for a second tour beginning 30 May 2001 in Scotland, before travelling south to venues including London's Almeida Theatre, who co-produced the tour. There were the following changes to the cast:

YOUNG CHRISSY, Martin Docherty

General Manager, Claire Robb
Company Stage Manager, Shona Wright

The first production was funded by the Scottish Arts Council's Scotland Onstage scheme, the second by the Arts Council of England and the Scottish Arts Council.

In 2010 Grid Iron remounted the play for a tenth anniversary production which toured in Scotland and England. The cast were:

DECKY, Ben Winger
DAVID, Martin McCormick
YOUNG CHRISSY, Gavin Wright
ADULT CHRISSY, John Kielty
YOUNG BARRY, Ross Allan
ADULT BARRY, Finn den Hertog
YOUNG O'NEILL, David Elliot
ADULT O'NEILL, Nicky Elliott

Set Build, Simon Owen
Stunt Co-ordinators, Lucy Deacon and Moritz Linkmann
Production Manager, Zoe Squair
Stage Manager, Nichola Reilly
Technical Manager, Ross McMillan

The tenth anniversary production was funded by Creative Scotland and Made in Scotland, which is part of the Scottish Government's Edinburgh Festivals Expo Fund.

Characters when children

DAVID

The narrator. Only seen as an adult. Joins in
kids' scenes as if he is the same age.

BARRY

His cousin. Old before his time and slightly
jealous of David's friendships.

DECKY

A very wee lad. Not sharp, but friendly and keen
to impress.

CHRISSY

A fiery fighter of a boy. Decky's best friend and
constant sparring partner.

O'NEIL

Popular and extremely good at any sport or
activity, looked up to by everyone.

Act One

Saturday Morning.

The lights come up behind The Swings. They are definitely centre stage and, when seen in silhouette like this, look like a huge scratchy alien spider. The swings themselves are barred. Someone has taken the time to throw them over the bar so many times that they cannot be reached from the ground unless you happen to be a giant, or a grown up of course. Four adults appear from behind the swings. They too are in silhouette and look like refugees from a close encounter. There is music. They run towards the swings and seem to fight with them. The adults are CHRISSY, BARRY, O'NEIL and DAVID. CHRISSY wears a boiler suit, BARRY a tie and a name badge and O'NEIL a leather jacket and a bandana. DAVID can wear whatever he wants. They twist round the poles, swing from the bar and noisily get the swings down from their twisted knots in time with the music. Once the swings are down they exit. DAVID steps forward. He sits on a swing for a moment and then addresses the audience directly, in a friendly, chatty manner.

DAVID: I used to live just down there. It was the third small white house to the right. All the houses on this part of the estate face in towards the wee hill, and the swings stand on top of that. It's almost as if the swings came first and stood alone for centuries until someone said 'You know what? Seeing as the swings are already here, we should build all the houses around them, so if there was ever an emergency the people can look out of any window and see the swings and everything will be alright.' And here they stand, to this very day, like a monument to all the brave chutes and climbing frames who gave their lives in the battle of Elder Avenue Swingpark long before you and I were even born. At first I lived in those flats there, but when I was one my mum and dad moved across the road in a house swap. For a while I thought they'd swapped the house for my wee sister, who suspiciously turned up when we arrived in the new house. I lived in the estate until we were eleven when my dad got promoted and we moved to a bigger place about five minutes away. Now they don't even live in the town anymore. Neither do I. Please don't get the wrong idea about Elder, it was a really nice council estate, or at least I thought so at the time. It was busy and clean. The place was absolutely teeming with dirty wee manky kids though. Hordes of the buggers, including myself of course, roamed the parks and gardens in massive swarms of bikes and bruises, trying to break the world record for the biggest ever game of British and Gerries. I've been in games of British and Gerries that involved more people than the Second World War.

By the summer of 1983, though, we had grown out of war games and graduated onto vandalism. Well, not really, but that's what it looked like to the army of nippy mothers watching the park for signs of the end of civilisation as they knew it. We had learned to Bronco. This is a Bronco...

(The adults enter at the back of the stage, run forward, grab the swings and worky up. DAVID talks over their swinging.)

DAVID: You worky up, put a foot behind the swings and bang!!!

(They Bronco. The swings fly over the bar, clanking and crashing. They go back and do it again to return the swings to their normal state.)

DAVID: Worky up... *(CRASH)* bang! God knows who discovered it, but what started off as vandalism ended up as a sport and completely took over the summer when I turned nine, filling the gap between Star Wars and football. I can't remember how we all got into the routine, but that's exactly what it was. Round about half-past nine every morning we'd all meet up at the swings. I was first because my house was nearest. I'd get the swings down from where the carry-out boys had barred then the night before in a moment of drunken violence and start jumping off. The swings were sticky rubber and usually wet with dew. The chains were rusted together for safety and left your hands brown and blistered after a hard day of life-threatening fun. Next to arrive was my cousin Barry.

(BARRY enters on a racing bike. Unless stated, the characters are the young versions, not their silent, grown up shadows. BARRY jumps off the bike but it speeds on to a violent, neglected crash. BARRY presses a button on his digital watch as if timing his arrival. He's not happy.)

BARRY: Oh no way!! No, no, no. I don't believe it. One minute short of the record. The traffic lights changed and I had to go over the pavement but a daft old woman got in the road. Is O'Neil coming the day?

DAVID: *(To audience.)* Barry came down from 'somewhere near Glasgow' every year and stayed with my Gran. For a number of complex reasons he was trying to get his journey from Gran's to my bit down to the lowest possible time. He had to be back for his tea at five, on the dot, or else he'd be executed or something, so he'd wait until exactly the shortest journey time before he left. He'd sit on his bike until exactly four minutes, 34 seconds to five, and the BOOM, he was off, leaving only a dust cloud and tyre tracks. I sometimes imagine what he must have looked like, bombing down the street at 50 miles an hour dodging in and out of confused civilians, caught up in a race they would never fully understand.

BARRY: What did you watch last night?

DAVID: *(Talks to BARRY and the others as if he is the same age.)* Matt Houston. Ace.

BARRY: Ace. Did you watch Dynasty?

DAVID: Nah.

BARRY: How come?

DAVID: D'know. It's rubbish.

BARRY: Are you not allowed to stay up?

DAVID: Aye!

BARRY: No yer no.

DAVID: Aye I um.

BARRY: No yer no. You're not allowed to stay up 'cause you burst out crying and wet the bed.

DAVID: No I don't! Jeezo Barry shut it.

BARRY: Boo hoo hooooo. Gi us a greet…mummy I've got heavy pants!!

DAVID: Shut it, I don't wet the… *(To audience.)* See this is typical. Barry's all right now, but see when he was wee, he could *really* wind me up. Just for the record, I've never wet the bed, that's just one of Barry's things.

BARRY: Big wimp.

(BARRY workys up and the Adult BARRY, in a tie and name badge, rolls underneath his moving swing. Young BARRY can't see him. Adult BARRY swings beside him and dodges Young BARRY during DAVID's speech.)

DAVID: It's funny how you end up, isn't it? Barry's totally different now. To everyone's surprise – including his I imagine – it turned out that he was really good looking. His adolescence was a dream. Lucky swine. We get on brilliantly now though. Meet up for the football or the occasional pint after work on a Friday. We're friends. But we don't talk about this. We don't talk about the story I'm going to tell you tonight. Probably because we don't want to…own it. We don't want to change it and make it our own, make it *mean* something. Because that's what happens when you look back. You put an adult frame around things. I think we give life a cause and effect that was never truly there.

(There is a blood-curdling scream offstage and it came from DECKY. DECKY runs on and weaves in and out of the poles and chains as if

he's being chased. As he passes, BARRY tries to kick him but misses. DECKY is very small and lacks the other lads' swing park abilities.)

DAVID: Decky!

DECKY: I'm going to get killed!

BARRY: Aye, off of me if you don't move it.

DECKY: No. Chrissy's going to kill me with a rope, 'cause I saved his life on the climbing frame.

DAVID: How's he going to kill you if you saved his life?

DECKY: He was sitting on top right? And I went up and said 'saved you life' and pushed him off.

DAVID: Aw, right. I see.

DECKY: Anyhow he's got a rope and he says he's going to…

(DECKY gives out another really high-pitched scream and points off stage. CHRISSY enters slowly and is swinging a huge fisherman's rope over his head like a lasso. There is a knot at the end and the weapon is at least the size of its owner. DECKY tears offstage in the opposite direction.)

CHRISSY: Decky!!! Decky I'm going to get you and kill you with this rope. *(Runs off after him.)* Now I am the master, ha ha ha!!!!!

DAVID: *(To audience.)* Perhaps I should explain. Decky and Chrissy were next door neighbours and best friends. They were always together and round each other's house but, and I can't stress this too strongly, they were always fighting. ALWAYS. Not verbal fights like me and Barry, but real physical fights that would last for days on end. No one could keep up with what the fight was about and they could only be stopped when it was teatime or bedtime. In the morning Decky would go round to Chrissy's house and pounce on him when he answered the door. At any given time of the day you could look out your window to the hill and see them wrestling in the muck like epileptic Siamese twins.

(The pair run on and then off again, CHRISSY still brandishing the rope. Adult CHRISSY comes forward and does a similar dance around the swing as Adult BARRY, only more reckless and dangerous looking. He jumps and Broncos, spins and punches before reluctantly exiting.)

DAVID: Last time I heard Chrissy was a mechanic, but I'm not even sure of that. He was one of those people who went from physically being a wee kid to being an adult within days. He just got huge. He also stopped saying hello to me in the street, obeying that secret instinctive code of who's 'all right' and who isn't, when you're a teenager. That disappears when you start drinking in pubs and you re-group with people as if they've been abroad for three years. I suppose they have. A three year break in 'Hard Land'. But that's years away.

(CHRISSY runs on in terror. In his short break from the stage he seems to have lost the rope. DECKY stalks on, swinging the beast with great difficulty and laughing like a cartoon villain.)

DECKY: Now *I* am the master!!

CHRISSY: Hit me wi' that rope and I'm no joking, I'll get a gun and shoot you in your bed.

DECKY: I am the master!

CHRISSY: I'll grass you up.

DECKY: Say 'I am the master'.

CHRISSY: I am the master.

DECKY: No, say '*I* am the master'.

CHRISSY: *I* am the master.

DECKY: Oooh you're dead.

(Suddenly CHRISSY makes a dash for BARRY's bike and hoists it above his head.)

BARRY: Ho!!!!!! *(Leaps off the swing and picks up a stone aimed at CHRISSY's head.)* Put the bike down ya wee maggot.

CHRISSY: Tell him to put the rope down.

DAVID: Put it down Decky.

DECKY: Nut. *(Less sure.)* I am the master.

(And before you know it we are in the midst of a Mexican stand-off of Tarantino proportions. CHRISSY screams and throws the bike at DECKY, BARRY chucks his stone simultaneously and CHRISSY hits the ground. BARRY runs to the bike and checks it for injuries. DAVID goes to DECKY.)

CHRISSY: That stone hit me in the lug.

BARRY: *(Screaming.)* If you bust the speedometer on this I'm going to get the police on you!

DAVID: Decky's dead.

(And right enough DECKY lies perfectly still under the bike.)

CHRISSY: I never did it.

BARRY: Aye you did, I saw you.

CHRISSY: It's your bike.

BARRY: So? You chucked it.

CHRISSY: No I never.

(CHRISSY bolts off stage. DECKY takes this as his cue and springs to his feet, grabs the rope and follows after him laughing.)

DECKY: I am the master!

DAVID: Is it bust?

BARRY: Naw, but it could of been. I hate them.

DAVID: Who? Decky and Chrissy?

BARRY: Aye. You shouldnae be hanging about with wee guys like that.

DAVID: Decky's the same age as me. Chrissy's all right.

BARRY: Aye but they're three years younger than me. I'm going to the high school next year, I won't be hanging about with wee guys like that.

DAVID: *(Under breath.)* Find your own pals then.

BARRY: *(Shouting.)* What?

DAVID: Nothing. Just that if you hate them so much, you shouldnae come down every summer.

BARRY: Grow up.

(DECKY and CHRISSY walk back on sadly punching each other's arm. They are minus the rope.)

BARRY: You bust my speedometer.

CHRISSY: Who?

BARRY: You.

DAVID: Where's the rope?

CHRISSY: *(Concerned.)* Maybe my dad can fix it, he's an inventor.

BARRY: It's all right, I'll fix it myself.

DAVID: Where's the rope?

DECKY: They guys took it from us.

DAVID: Who?

DECKY: O'Neil's big brother and that.

CHRISSY: Aye, took it from you, you mean. You're too wee. If I'd been carrying it they wouldnae have got it. Coming we'll all go down there and get it back?

(There is a pause as they imagine what horrors would await them.)

BARRY: What do you want a stupid rope for anyway? Grow up.

CHRISSY: David? Come on, they'll give it back to you, your dad's a teacher.

DECKY: I'm no going. They'll go for me first, they always do.

DAVID: Aye, Decky's right. Maybe when O'Neil gets here he'll just ask for it back.

CHRISSY: When O'Neil gets here me and him'll go down there and batter them.

(CHRISSY goes to a swing and workys up sitting down. BARRY does the same. DECKY stands at the poles and watches. DAVID goes over the join him.)

DAVID: You going to jump off today?

DECKY: Dunno.

DAVID: You should do it, it's ace. We can all Bronco now and you cannae even jump off.

DECKY: I did it once but no one was here.

DAVID: How did you?

DECKY: I did. I came up here in the middle of the night and tried it and I done it. It was better in the dark and I bet it was much scarier than now.

DAVID: Do it now then.

DECKY: Nut.

(CHRISSY and BARRY are now at the bumps.)

CHRISSY: *(Shouting to BARRY.)* First one to jump off, back and Bronco!

BARRY: Right… GO!

(They go into a race. BARRY jumps first, followed by CHRISSY. They go back and Bronco. BARRY is determined and may cheat a little. Whoever wins on the night, celebrates in an over-exaggerated manner

and the loser complains bitterly about the cheating and demands a rematch. DECKY takes over a swing and slowly workys up.)

CHRISSY: Here he goes.

BARRY: That's my swing you!

DAVID: Jump off Decky!

CHRISSY: Jump Decky ya wee chicken

BARRY: Get off that swing!

DAVID: Jump!!

(He jumps but only takes one hand off of the chains. He clings to the swing as he comes scraping to a halt on the ground.)

CHRISSY: Ha ha, he never let go.

DAVID: That's probably more dangerous than just jumping off on to the grass.

BARRY: Serves you right for nicking my swing.

DECKY: Sorry Barry.

BARRY: That's all right. I don't care, it's only a swing.

(BARRY grabs the swing with a passion and begins workying up. CHRISSY is practising a handstand which is at the 'kicking your feet up' stage.)

DECKY: I've hurt my knee.

CHRISSY: Look!

DECKY: I was going to do it but I saw a stone…and some dog turd.

CHRISSY: Look!

DAVID: *(Bored with DECKY's excuses.)* You should just do it. What'll you do when we're all Broncoing?

CHRISSY: You missed it. I was doing a handstand there for about five minutes.

BARRY: O'Neil's coming!!!

(DAVID and CHRISSY climb up the poles for a look. DECKY jumps up now and then with no real benefit.)

DECKY: He's no got anyone with him has he?

DAVID: *(From wherever he happens to be hanging, to the audience.)* Decky always had a paranoid fear of O'Neil's pals. As far as I knew he'd never even met any of O'Neil's pals, but he'd somehow convinced himself that a legion of hard men and psychos were going to turn up and ask if they could stay in his house or something. I think, more realistically, he was scared O'Neil would bring even more athletic, good looking people who could jump off swings, which could only add to his daily failure.

(Enter O'NEIL. He walks slowly with only a nod of recognition in response to the voluminous greeting he gets from the lads. He goes to a swing and expertly workys up. Adult O'NEIL appears and jumps on the same swing as young O'NEIL. They go through some ace acrobatics as DAVID speaks. All the boys move away from the swings in awe.)

DAVID: *(To audience.)* O'Neil, as if I had to tell you, was one of those naturally cool people. A lot of this coolness was to do with his amazing sporting abilities. Not just real sports, but stuff like this as well. He was a national champion at tree climbing, diving into the harbour and sliding down hills on bits of cardboard. I also believe he made the Winter Olympic team for skiteing his bike across a frozen burn. I've no idea what he's doing now. We all thought he was going to be a professional footballer. Another small town disaster. He got a girl called Louise pregnant round about the same time as I was struggling to understand the offside rule. He always knew more about the world than any of us, that's probably why he didn't say too much.

(Adult O'NEIL leaves in a dramatic jump.)

O'NEIL: Line up. I'm going to do 4.

CHRISSY: Bags going first!

(There is a mad scramble as the boys lie on the ground in front of O'NEIL's swing. DAVID reluctantly lies furthest away.)

DAVID: *(To audience.)* You notice the lack of doubt in the air? Oh well. *(To O'NEIL.)* O'Neil? You done this before? *(No response.)* O'Neil?

CHRISSY: That's how I'm not lying there. Last time he landed on wee Andy and he had to be carried home greetin'.

(DECKY makes a break for it but is pulled down by CHRISSY and after a few exchanged punches settles down.)

O'NEIL: Sit down Decky ya dick.

BARRY: Aye, sit down Decky ya dick. Who was wee Andy?

DAVID: What do you mean *was?* He wasn't killed was he?

CHRISSY: He's the wee guy that keeps getting his bike nicked.

BARRY: I hate him.

DAVID: What a surprise.

O'NEIL: I'm jumping here!

(DECKY seems to be leaking a low groan of terror as O'NEIL jumps. He's high up, the jump is spectacular and he clears them all with ease.)

O'NEIL: Yes!! Did you see that? I'm ace, man. None of yous could do that, no way. Who else can we get and I'll do 5.

BARRY: Get David's wee sister.

DAVID: Oh now come on.

CHRISSY: We could lie out long ways.

O'NEIL: Aye!

DAVID: Look, let's just have a big race instead.

BARRY: Aye. GO!!

(BARRY races off. The others call him back.)

OTHERS: Wait! Wait!

CHRISSY: Is it normal rules or Indian rules?

O'NEIL: Indian rules.

CHRISSY: We've got no nails but.

DAVID: I don't like it when we use nails anyway.

BARRY: Don't race then!

CHRISSY: Make it if you touch the chains folk can do anything they want to you.

(They give DECKY a bloodthirsty look.)

CHRISSY: Okay so it's up to the top, back down, go to the side.

O'NEIL: Naw. Go round once, back, Bronco. If you touch the chains you got to go back to the start.

BARRY· Right. So it's up, down, along, along, through, up to the top, back round, chains, jump, Bronco, chains, back, jump and back.

(Impatiently, they agree, except DECKY who is nowhere near understanding.)

O'NEIL: GO!!

(DANCE. This is the boys' morning shown in dance. The adults also take part. The boys are racing, DECKY and CHRISSY fighting and O'NEIL performing more and more elaborate jumps. What must also be shown is the adult relationships with their younger halves. For instance, BARRY is successful now and not at all the difficult child he was, so he may wish to reprimand Young BARRY for cheating and starting trouble. Adult O'NEIL may regret some of the choices he made in life and sees this as his chance to stop showing off and acting up. Adult CHRISSY misses the fun and carefree messing about of his youth, so he actively encourages Young CHRISSY in his fights and games. DAVID is part of the kids race and for the sake of the dance, he is a child. For reasons that will become clear later, the adults are keen to play with DECKY where the boys never notice

that they're actively ignoring him. The choreographer has free reign, but the section should be a real spectacle with people in the air at all times and swings crashing over the music. The section ends with a race which O'NEIL [of course] wins. Second is BARRY followed closely by DAVID, then CHRISSY. The Adults leave the stage and the boys sit on the ground having a break. Well not all of them. After a minute or so it becomes clear to them that DECKY is still running the race. He's so far behind that it looks like a new race, but he's not giving up. Of course, the difficulty is that he can't jump off swings; so every time a jump is required he goes through the cling-fall-scrape routine as before.)

DAVID: Decky, what are you doing?

DECKY: *(Panting and spluttering.)* I'm running the race.

(They all laugh.)

CHRISSY: Decky ya wee dick, the race's finished.

O'NEIL: I won. Decky it's over. *(Shouting.)* I won!!

BARRY: *(To O'NEIL.)* That was an ace turn you did when you jumped off at the end.

O'NEIL: I know man, I just went… *(Mimes it out in slow motion with sound effects.)*

DAVID: I did that an all.

BARRY: No you never. You don't even Bronco properly.

CHRISSY: *(Fascinated by DECKY's marathon of pain.)* Look at wee Decky. Ha ha ha!

DAVID: What do you mean? I do it the same way as yous.

BARRY: No you don't, you do this. *(Another slow-motion mime.)*

DAVID: No I don't, I do this *(He joins in the miming. Now the sound effects are loud and sound more like a massacre than a Bronco competition.)*

DECKY: *(Coming over and lying flat on his face.)* Done it. I done it.

CHRISSY: *(Kicks him.)* It doesnae count if you don't Bronco.

DECKY: *(Devastated.)* What? Naeone telt us that. What are they doing?

CHRISSY: David doesnae Bronco properly, so says Barry.

DECKY: *(In conspiratory whispers with CHRISSY.)* I hate that Barry. We should get'm.

CHRISSY: How but?

DECKY: Did you see Dukes of Hazard last night?

CHRISSY: Aye, that's an ace idea, we put him in a car and push him off a cliff.

DECKY: No! We go down to Shanty Shaws, tie a knot in the big grass, right? And then we get him down there, chase him, and he'll trip.

CHRISSY: That's nothing.

DECKY: *(Thinks.)* Well…we could put stones down where he'll fall.

CHRISSY: Right. Don't tell David though, you know what he's like.

DECKY: Right. He'd just tell Barry. Do you think he likes Barry better than us?

CHRISSY: He likes me better than you.

DECKY: No he doesnae, he likes me better than you.

CHRISSY: Your mum likes me better than you.

DECKY: Least I've got a mum.

(A fight starts. Quite a serious one. The others stop their own squabble over Broncoing technique to watch.)

DAVID: Split it up.

BARRY: Let them fight. You're always stopping things.

DECKY: *(Like Batfink.)* You can't harm me. My wings are like a shield of steel.

(DECKY and CHRISSY exit.)

O'NEIL: Hey, I was in a fight last night.

(DAVID and BARRY are more interested in O'NEIL.)

BARRY: Who with?

O'NEIL: Hannah.

BARRY: Who's she?

DAVID: Gary Hannah. He's thirteen.

BARRY: So. I'll be thirteen soon.

DAVID: We'll all be thirteen someday. *(Makes a long suffering 'see what I mean' face at the audience.)*

O'NEIL: I was down the Horse Rocks diving in last night.

DAVID: Last night? I'm not even allowed down there in the daytime.

BARRY: If I lived down here I'd be allowed.

O'NEIL: Well me and my brother were diving in an' that. Hannah was there with some lassies and one of them got stuck in the seaweed, so I just swan over there and ripped her free. She was like 'Oh you're a total hero', and kissed me and everything. Hannah was fuming man and started fighting me. I totally panned him. He was greetin'. I'm going back tonight, that lassie might be there. You can come if you want.

DAVID: There's no way I'd be allowed.

BARRY: Aye you would. It's just that we're doing something else.

O'NEIL: What?

BARRY: We're going out with lassies.

DAVID: What??

O'NEIL: Oh right. I see. Nice one.

(O'NEIL goes back to the swings, a tad jealous. DAVID takes BARRY aside.)

DAVID: Are you mental? Why did you say that?

BARRY: You shouldnae say you arenae allowed to do stuff. It makes you sound like a big baby.

DAVID: But why did you say we were going out with girls, I hate girls, man. What if he asks us about it?

BARRY: I'll handle it, Jeezo.

(Their attention goes back to the featherweight bout of the year, which continues in front of them.)

BARRY: What's this one about, who's the biggest tube?

DAVID: Dunno. Split it up yous, it's nearly my lunchtime. Who wants to see who can do the best stunts?

O'NEIL: Me.

BARRY: Your mum's shouting you.

DAVID: So she is. I'll have to go in, right? Coming?

BARRY: Aye.

(BARRY takes his bike and walks it off. The fight instantly stops.)

CHRISSY: C'moan.

DECKY: Aye, this way!

DAVID: What are you two up to?

CHRISSY: *(Thinks.)* We're going looking for the van.

DECKY: Ice poles.

O'NEIL: Get me a couple right? I'll give you the money later.

CHRISSY: Eh…I think they'll be sold out.

DAVID: Then why are you going?

DECKY: *(Struggling.)* To get some.

CHRISSY: To get some to take them to the van so they don't run out again.

(They run off excited and impressed at the quality of their covering story.)

DAVID: What are you doing for lunch O'Neil?

O'NEIL: Dunno.

DAVID: I'll ask my mum if you can come to my bit if you want.

O'NEIL: Nah, it's all right. Think I'll go and find my brother.

(He jumps off his swing and exits.)

DAVID: No one had ever been to O'Neil's house. I wasn't even sure where he lived. Somewhere up the scheme, near the wee shop. There were four or five parks between there and here. But these were definitely O'Neil's swings. We were *very* territorial. A journey on the bikes down to the roundabout, or the Pine Quadrant grass was like a trip into a foreign country. We told each other to watch for traps, 'don't trust them, they're not like us down here'. Some of these heathens didn't even Bronco! Sometimes, if we were feeling especially adventurous we'd even go right across town to the big parks. This was dangerous because it involved crossing real roads and only O'Neil could boast permission from the commanding officers. I remember we all went on one of these wagon trains into injun country to track down a boy we'd heard tale of, who had swallowed his tongue while jumping off a swing. The people of his land informed us, in a strange unfamiliar dialect, that this was mere a legend created by the wise ones to neuter swing abuse. Legend or not, from now on we jumped with special attention to keeping our tongues in the right way round.

(Lights down.)

Saturday Afternoon.

(Lights up over the swings. The adults, including DAVID, enter slowly to music. They prowl around the swings. This is where we see their adult relationships to each other. BARRY and DAVID are friends, but there is an awkwardness between them. O'NEIL and CHRISSY too, but one minute they are taunting DAVID, the next they are friendly. O'NEIL is withdrawn, angry and bitter. CHRISSY is lethargic and sad. BARRY is a bit of a go-getter. Once again the choreographer has the right to decide exactly how long this piece should be, perhaps even just one tight sequence. They exit leaving DAVID alone on stage. He is about to speak when a burst of laughs machine gun in from offstage. It's BARRY and O'NEIL. They enter along with CHRISSY and DECKY. CHRISSY is helping DECKY along, because it looks as if he's injured. By his groans you'd think he had an ear missing, but all he has is a bleeding nose. O'NEIL and BARRY can't stand up for laughing and clutch their sides. CHRISSY's trying, for the sake of his friend, to hold in his giggles.)

DAVID: Decky! What happened? Were you in a fight? Hold your head back.

BARRY: *(Through his laughter.)* No, hold it forward, my mum's a nurse.

DAVID: Your mum is not a nurse.

BARRY: So?

(DECKY decides to compromise and rocks backwards and forwards like a bloodstained Stevie Wonder.)

O'NEIL: Oh man, that was a peach. You should have seen it!

DAVID: What happened?

DECKY: *(Mutters something incoherent.)*…eghft, …bantum, frupping stones.

DAVID: What?

BARRY: You missed yourself man, funniest thing I've seen in ages.

DAVID: Chrissy, tell me!

CHRISSY: Me and Decky were down at Shanty Shaws right and we shouted to Barry to come and see this thing…

BARRY: What was it by the way?

CHRISSY: Oh it was away by then.

BARRY: Aye, but what was it?

CHRISSY: *(In trouble.)* Eh…it wis…a…bike.

BARRY: A Bike? How would I want to see a bike?

CHRISSY: Just. It was ace. What a bike man!

DAVID: Will somebody tell me what happened to Decky before I start breaking faces.

O'NEIL: We were all down at Shanty Shaws and my brother and that jumped us. *(Laughs.)*

DAVID: Hilarious.

O'NEIL: They had this big rope right? We totally bombed it up the slope and hid behind the bricks. Barry goes…

BARRY: I goes 'C'moan we'll pelt them wi stones and attack them. 1-2-3-go!' and Decky thought I was serious and…

O'NEIL: Decky thought he was serious and flew down the hill, shouting all this stuff and waving his arms about an' everything. *(More laughing.)*

DAVID: So you got a doing off a O'Neil's brother?

CHRISSY: *(Shakes his head sadly.)* Na

DECKY: *(Shakes his head sadly.)* Nfght.

BARRY: He never made it that far. He got into the long grass and WHOOSH, down he goes.

O'NEIL: Someone had tied the grass in a loop and put stones down! Imagine that. What an ace trap. It must have been my brother. Ha ha.

CHRISSY: Aye…imagine that. *(Gives DECKY a disapproving look.)*

BARRY: I got stung by nettles down there.

DAVID: Put a whatdoyicallit on it. A Dock leaf.

BARRY: It's a dochen leaf ya spazy.

(All of the boys sit in front of the swings.)

DAVID: So?

CHRISSY: How come is it that they leafs grow right next to the nettles?

BARRY: *(Making a biff face.)* I'm a biff!!! So that when you sting yourself you use them to take the sting away.

CHRISSY: But how? How did the plants know?

DECKY: *(Stopped bleeding now.)* God put them together for our convenience.

O'NEIL: Aw naw! Don't tell us you believe in God?

DECKY: Nut.

O'NEIL: If there was a God, he'd mix the nettles and the dock leaves in one plant so that as soon as you'd get stung you'd get the sting rubbed off.

CHRISSY: You believe in God don't you David 'cause you're a pape.

DAVID: Just because you're Catholic doesn't mean you believe in God.

CHRISSY: Protestants don't believe in God.

BARRY: What do you mean? I know hunners of Protestants that believe in God.

O'NEIL: Who?

BARRY: *(Thinks.)* The minister must believe in God or else he'd get fired.

CHRISSY: Ach, that doesnae count, 'cause all ministers are Catholic.

DAVID: What even the Protestant ones?

CHRISSY: Catholic means churches and praying an' that. If you do all that you're Catholic and if you stay at home and stuff, that means you're a Protestant.

BARRY: You're so thick man.

CHRISSY: Shut your face you!

BARRY: Or what?

CHRISSY: I'll pan it.

O'NEIL: Oooh Chrissy's hard.

DECKY: Maybe we need to get stung.

EVERYONE: What?

DECKY: I mean, if we never got stung, we wouldnae need the dock leafs. They'd just sit there doing nothing. We'd never even see them.

(Everyone laughs at DECKY.)

BARRY: We're no even talking about that now. Grow up.

O'NEIL: Decky, you're so thick it's untrue.

DECKY: No I'm no.

CHRISSY: How come you need a special teacher then?

(And surprise surprise a fight breaks out. It starts out seriously between DECKY and CHRISSY but turns toy when BARRY and O'NEIL decide to join in. A chase-fight-chase situation ensues.)

CHRISSY: *(Piggyback on O'NEIL.)* When we first met, I was the pupil and you were the master. Now I am the master.

DECKY: *(Piggyback on BARRY.)* I am defenceless. Take your weapon. Strike me down. And your journey to the dark side will be complete.

(They exit, running. DAVID steps forward and talks to the audience.)

DAVID: Ah, happy, peaceful days. I'm a pathological reminiscer. I was reminiscing about lost days of youth when I was still a child, really. We'd come up here and sit at the swings late at night after a community centre teenage disco and reminisce about our lost distant days of youth. Community centre discos! They were grim, nerve-wracking affairs. The boys would pretend to be bored on one side of the room and the girls would pretend to be bored on the other. Occasionally we'd meet in the middle for some stumbling, but mostly it was the bored thing. Anyway, after a hard night of pretending to be drunk on coke with aspirin in it, we'd come up here, reminisce and get ironic. They should warn about the dangers of irony in schools you know. It was the same old story; a bit of cheek in the classroom just to be social. Then I moved to sarcasm – I needed a bigger hit. Before I knew it I was being ironic first thing in the morning.

O'NEIL: David, c'moan. We're all going to worky up on the same swing. Wait til I put it round the right way.

(The boys' fight has stopped and an organised game has taken its place. DAVID joins them as they start this record-breaking attempt. Everyone but the adults get on the same swing.)

CHRISSY: Decky should get on first seeing he's the wee-est.

(He does as he's told, standing uncomfortably and gripping the chains for dear life.)

O'NEIL: David you go on that side Barry this side.

(The wingers go on.)

CHRISSY: I'll go on the front facing you.

O'NEIL: And I'll go behind you.

(They're all on and set for take off.)

O'NEIL: Worky up!

BARRY: Worky up!

(They all jiggle and sway the swing but there is no forward motion.)

DAVID: *(Shouting.)* Jeezo! All go the same way.

(They stop.)

O'NEIL: Ready? 1-2-3. Go!

(Exactly the same movements. The adults appear on the stage and slowly move to the swing. They give the boys a gentle push. Music starts. The boys all cheer as they gather speed. The music quickens with the swing. The adults seem keen to scare the boys. There are shouts from BARRY and DAVID to slow down. DECKY starts to scream.)

O' NEIL: Jump off! Jump off!

(Everyone falls off the swing. The music is now at full tilt as the boys all leap off the swings in a messy and sore-looking crash. A terrified DECKY stays on and the adults help him off. Everyone seems to be okay, except DAVID who is lying on the ground crying. The adults exit after making sure that DECKY is all right. The boys crowd round DAVID, genuinely concerned.)

BARRY: Are you okay?

O'NEIL: That looked a sore one.

CHRISSY: David? Do you want us tae get your mum?

BARRY: I'll get her, he's my cousin.

DAVID: *(Through tears and holding his chest.)* Naw, naw. I'm all right. I cannae breathe but.

DECKY: What happened?

(DAVID is helped up by the other kids.)

O'NEIL: He's winded. Take big breaths.

(They all take a big breath.)

DECKY: What's 'windowed'?

CHRISSY: Winded!

DAVID: I landed right on my chest *(Calming down.)* I'm all right now. I might go home.

BARRY: *(Nicely.)* Don't go home David. You'll be okay in a couple of minutes.

DECKY: Aye stay. Sit over here.

(DECKY, BARRY and CHRISSY sit to the side of the swings. O'NEIL goes back to the swings and does a few Broncos.)

O'NEIL: That was a total cracker man! Whack! AAAAhhhhh!!!

DAVID: *(Laughing.)* I know. I thought I was dead there.

CHRISSY: See when I fell off the ambulance station, I thought I was dead then.

BARRY: I was nearly killed once. I was bombing across this road along from my house and a motorbike totally flew past me about that far away. *(Holds up his fingers about a millimetre apart.)* and I was shaking after it.

DECKY: I think if you're our age it's harder to get killed.

BARRY: No it's no, it's easier. Think about it, when you're older you've got muscles to protect you…

CHRISSY: And guns.

BARRY: And guns.

DECKY: Aye but, like look at Crawfy. He fell out of his flat window and landed in a skip that was miles down, and *he* only broke his back. But if my mum fell out of a flat into a skip I bet you she'd die.

CHRISSY: You'd be better making sure you didn't live that far above a skip. When I grow up I'm going to live in America with my mum.

(BARRY and DAVID exchange glances.)

DAVID: Where abouts in America does your mum live?

CHRISSY: Eh, I think it's Hollywood or New York. My dad used to work in Richmond Virginia before he left to come back over here to be an inventor. He worked in a factory.

BARRY: What does your dad invent?

DAVID: That bogie! You've seen it. You know that ace one with suspension and brakes. It's the best bogie I've ever seen.

CHRISSY: I know. I'm the fastest n'all. Come on we'll get the bogies out?

DECKY: Mine's is bust. I crashed it.

DAVID: What are you going to be when you grow up Decky?

BARRY: A midget. I'm going to be a journalist.

DECKY: Naw, I'm going to be in the army.

O'NEIL: *(Like BA from A Team.)* Shut up fool. You're too wee to be in the army.

DECKY: No I'm no, they take anyone. I saw it on a programme and it was America right? This wee guy ran away after fighting with his dad and joined up.

DAVID: Aye, that's America but.

DECKY: So. I'm going any day now.

(They all laugh. CHRISSY can't resist giving DECKY a small Chinese burn.)

DECKY: I'm no joking. See if I just go away, I'll be in the army. If my old boy gives me any grief I'll just say, 'See ya! I'm going to join the army, get a gun and come back and shoot you in the legs'.

O'NEIL: *(Jumps off the swing.)* This is boring. Are yous not coming for a Bronco?

DAVID: It'll be my tea soon. I might just go in. What time is it anyway?

O'NEIL: About ten past five.

(BARRY screams, looks at his watch, sprints to his bike and pedals offstage in the fastest exit theatre has ever seen. The boys look to the space where BARRY used to be.)

O'NEIL: What's up with him?

DAVID: He has to get back to my Gran's before five or else he turns into a pumpkin.

CHRISSY: But if it's ten past, then he'll need to go back in time.

DAVID: Well he was going pretty fast...

O'NEIL: I'm away as well. I'm going to the chippy for my tea. Are yous coming out to the Horse Rocks tonight?

(They all shake their heads.)

O'NEIL: Aw well...see yous the morra.

(O'NEIL exits whistling happily.)

CHRISSY: O'Neil never goes home.

DECKY: He must go home at night.

DAVID: He probably likes being outside.

CHRISSY: My dad's forever chucking me out of the house. He says that watching TV makes you thick.

DAVID: How can it make you thick? I think you learn hunners of stuff. I wish you could just stay in and watch TV all day. That's what I'm going to do when I'm in my own house.

DECKY: I don't want to learn any more stuff. I know everything already. I'm full up.

CHRISSY: How do you? You cannae even Bronco.

DAVID: They don't let you in the army unless you're good at swings.

DECKY: Shut up.

DAVID: It's true. Make it there's a war and then you parachute down in a German swing park. What then?

DECKY: *(Less sure.)* Shut up.

CHRISSY: I've got an idea. Coming we'll teach Decky to Bronco.

DECKY: I can Bronco already, just I cannae be bothered doing it.

(DAVID and CHRISSY laugh.)

DAVID: Go then.

DECKY: Nut.

CHRISSY: Bronco or I'll kill you.

DECKY: Nut, I'm going in for my tea.

DAVID: *(Chanting.)* Decky cannae Bronco, Decky cannae Bronco…etc.

(CHRISSY joins in and they start clapping. This looks as if it's really upsetting DECKY. He puts his hands over his ears. The chanting becomes faster and mutates into an 'Oi, oi, oi, oi…' thing. DECKY has had enough and streaks over to the swings, jumps on, and starts workying up. DAVID and CHRISSY stop and watch. The music begins. The adults appear at the back of the stage: just watching. DECKY goes to Bronco but can't go through with it. He scrapes the swing to a halt and is crying. DAVID and CHRISSY don't realise how upset he is. They laugh.)

DECKY: *(Shouting in fury.)* Okay so I cannae Bronco, I don't care. Yous are better at things than me and I don't care. I hate swings anyway. I hate swings and I hate yous. It's not nice to laugh at folks who arenae as good as you. Well you can keep your daft swings, I don't care. I'm never coming back so you won't have to worry. I've got other pals. I'm going to the army and I'm never coming back. I'm never coming back!!

(DECKY runs off stage. CHRISSY instinctively runs after him. The adults move threateningly in towards DAVID.)

DAVID: *(To audience.)* If I'm telling this story…If I'm shaping it, like I said earlier on; why can't I go after Decky now and say that I'm sorry? Why can't I tell him that this summer at the swings is just a way of getting by? It's a game. Why can't I stop the story here and make things better? Stop time in its tracks. Why? Because this is for me. Not for Decky. To take me *away*. To cure me. To stop me looking for him every time I see a crowd of kids playing at the swings. How was I meant to know? Eh? How was I meant to know that on that very night as I was tucked up safe in my bed that Decky had finished his childhood. How was I to know that? But I know now. And I'll tell you one thing that's certain…he's never coming back.

(Music and lights down.)

End of Act One.

ACT TWO

Sunday Morning.

(Lights up through the music and over the swings. One swing is Broncoed, the others are calmly down. The big difference is that they have been cordoned off by Police Incident tape. The swings look like an exhibit in an art gallery. CHRISSY enters with his hands in his pockets looking a bit lost. When he sees the tape around the swings he double takes, mutters to himself and then casually starts unwinding it. Enter DAVID.)

CHRISSY: *(Entering.)* Monkey magic, monkey magic…etc. Pigsy…I can hear you. I can smell you…

DAVID: What's going on?

CHRISSY: God knows. Some biff's been mucking about with this tape stuff.

DAVID: Maybe it was the police?

CHRISSY: Oh aye, they're arresting the swings!

(They sing the Professionals theme tune.)

DAVID: 'Anything you say may be taken down and Broncoed'. Decky no with you?

CHRISSY: Na. Wee dick. I went round his house, right? And no one answered for ages, then this woman came to the door and she was greetin'.

DAVID: What for?

CHRISSY: Dunno. Maybe *The Waltons* was on.

DAVID: Did you see Decky last night?

CHRISSY: Naw, he bombed it off.

DAVID: His dad was round at my bit this morning.

CHRISSY: How?

DAVID: Dunno. My mum was like 'who else does Decky play with?'

CHRISSY: No way! I'll bet he's run away.

DAVID: That's what I thought. He wouldnae would he?

CHRISSY: I'll bet he's run away 'cause of what we said last night.

DAVID: *(Panicking.)* Right! See if anyone asks, we didnae do anything, right? He just went home. Don't even tell Barry or O'Neil if they ask. If it's our fault we could get in real trouble man.

CHRISSY: Spit.

(They spit on their hands and shake. CHRISSY puts an end of the tape in his mouth and mumbles something incoherent.)

DAVID: What?

CHRISSY: *(Removes tape.)* I said wrap this tape stuff round us. *(Tape back in mouth.)*

(DAVID takes the other end and slowly maypoles CHRISSY who soon resembles a small mummy.)

DAVID: I mean, surely he hasnae went off to join the army? Where would he go? Where's the nearest army place? They won't let him in, no-matter what he says. They didnae even let him in the Cubs. He's far too wee. He'll probably turn up at the army and they'll phone his mum and dad. 'Member when thingby's big sister ran away? They had the police out and everything. Everyone thought she was going to have a baby and that a teacher was the dad. It turned out she was just fat. I knew that anyway. She got all the way to Ayr mind you, so she couldnae have been that daft. Decky'll get nowhere near Ayr, he's far too wee. Aw naw, man we're in big trouble. The police'll want to ask us stuff. My dad'll kill me. Aw naw…

(Suddenly BARRY enters in the same finishing line style as Act One. He lets the bike crash down as he leaps off. He is ecstatic.)

BARRY: Yeeeeessssss!!!!! Yeeha! I done it. I've done it! Ya dancer!

(He jumps on and off a swing in a little dance of triumph.)

BARRY: I did it. Three minutes and 56 seconds. Oh it was like a dream; no traffic, no pedestrians, green lights. Oh man. I'm in heaven. Well, say something.

DAVID: Congratulations.

BARRY: I know. Wait till I tell O'Neil about it. That means I'll be able to stay later the day.

DAVID: 37 seconds later.

BARRY: They all count in the long run.

DAVID: Notice anything different?

BARRY: What?

DAVID: Look around.

BARRY: Oh aye…Chrissy's dressed up as a mummy.

DAVID: Decky's no here.

CHRISSY: Ho…I thought we werenae meant to say anything about that?

DAVID: *(Whispering.)* Naw, we can say about that but not about me and you and Decky. Right?

BARRY: What?

DAVID: Nothing.

BARRY: So what's the big deal? Decky's no here, so what?

DAVID: We think he's run away. This woman was crying round his house an' his old boy was round my bit this morning.

BARRY: So. That's nothing. He'll be up the back road. How come he's wrapped up in that stuff.

DAVID: It was round the swings.

CHRISSY: I'm going to jump off the big hill.

(CHRISSY hops offstage. BARRY follows.)

BARRY: I'm coming 'n all.

CHRISSY: No! You'll push me.

BARRY: How will I? Anyway, you're jumping!

CHRISSY: That's a totally different thing.

(They both exit.)

DAVID: *(To audience.)* Decky was gone and was big news. And I've got to admit, I was a bit jealous. Jealous of Decky? Well…I'd always envied the rows he got from his mum and dad. When I would be getting morally reprimanded and boiled in guilt, he'd be learning reams of new swear words and baffling phrases that would impress his friends and raise his social profile. Once, Decky and me took all these tools from a tractor that was cutting the grass. We weren't going to sell them or anything, we just wanted to take apart the TV and climb in. Holy Lord in heaven did we get into trouble that night. Decky's dad really whacked him; swear words ablazing. I wonder if he remembers that?

(Enter Adult O'NEIL. He acts and speaks like Young O'NEIL. He sits on a swing and puts his head in his hands. The other actors speak to him as if he is still Young O'NEIL.)

DAVID: All right? *(No answer.)* O'Neil? What's up?

O'NEIL: Nothing.

DAVID: *(Sitting on the next swing along.)* Guess what?

O'NEIL: What?

DAVID: Decky's ran away.

O'NEIL: *(Visibly shocked. He groans.)*

DAVID: It's ace isn't it. He's bombed it up to Ayr, to the army base 'cause his dad was shouting at him.

O'NEIL: *(Keen.)* Has he? How do you know? Do you know for sure?

DAVID: Well some woman was crying when Chrissy went round and his dad was at my house the day.

O'NEIL: So? What is all that stuff about the army?

DAVID: Well that's obvious. Oh, and there was tape all round the swings this morning. We think it might have been the police that done it.

O'NEILL: Na, it cannae be the police, 'cause McPutty was round at my bit all morning and he's the only police we've got.

DAVID: How come he was round at your mum's?

O'NEIL: He wasnae. He was at my real dad's. That's where I've been staying.

DAVID: When did your real dad get back?

O'NEIL: Last week. *(Broncos.)*

(There is a pause as DAVID works out things in his head. O'NEIL isn't swinging.)

DAVID: How come McPutty was round at your real dad's?

O'NEIL: How do I know? I think he's helping them solve a case again.

(O'NEIL wraps the swing again.)

DAVID: Wow. I thought you werenae allowed to stay at your dad's.

(O'NEIL shrugs.)

DAVID: So what do you think about Decky?

O'NEIL: *(Angrily.)* I don't care about that wee dick! What was he doing up at the swings if he cannae Bronco anyroads? And he'd never be able to do this...

(O'NEIL Broncos the swing with such force that it wraps itself right to the bar.)

O'NEIL: I'd like to see him try that. All of his life he's never even done nothing as beautiful as that.

DAVID: What's up with you?

(BARRY and CHRISSY enter. CHRISSY is hobbling.)

CHRISSY: He pushed me right down the big hill. I was like that 'Aaaaahhhhh!!'

BARRY: All right O'Neil? I never pushed him, he was jumping.

CHRISSY: Aye, I was going to jump at the grassy bit, not over the stones.

BARRY: What difference does it make?

CHRISSY: I wish you'd just get lost sometimes.

BARRY: Don't get at me 'cause your little pal's gone.

CHRISSY: Shut it!

BARRY: He's probably ran away because you kept fighting him like a wee baby all the time.

CHRISSY: I'm going to pan you if you don't shut it.

DAVID: Aye, Barry give it a rest. It's got nothing to do with Chrissy.

BARRY: I'm surprised he didnae do it before now. If you were always bothering me I'd have packed my bags and hopped it to America years ago.

CHRISSY: I never bothered him, it was a game. You don't even know anything about it. He's my best friend.

BARRY: Oh aye, some best friend. Did he say goodbye then, when he ran away? No. If that's what best friends are like, then I don't want one.

CHRISSY: And you'll never have one either. That's how you always come down here at the summer, 'cause you've nae pals back wherever you come from.

BARRY: *(Shouting.)* Who says?

CHRISSY: David.

(BARRY spins round to face DAVID who is surprised and betrayed.)

BARRY: Well...David do you not like me coming here?

CHRISSY: Tell him.

DAVID: It's...it's not that I don't like you or that. It's just that we spend all day every day together...you're a good laugh and that...but...

BARRY: Right. It's okay. I don't care. I'll no bother you anymore. I'll phone my dad tonight and go home the morra.

CHRISSY: Cheerio.

BARRY: *(To CHRISSY.)* I hate you.

CHRISSY: I hate you worse.

BARRY: O'Neil? O'Neil? Do you hate me too?

DAVID: No one hates you Barry.

CHRISSY: Eh, hello, what did I just say? *I* hate him.

BARRY: O'Neil?

O'NEIL: *(Angry.)* What??

BARRY: Do you hate me?

O'NEIL: I don't care. What does it matter about me? Who cares what I think? They're all like that 'oh don't blame yourself' as if I would. I don't care. I hate everyone. No one's going to get me, no way.

BARRY: So do I. I hate everyone an' all.

(BARRY goes to his bike and walks it away. O'NEIL runs off.)

DAVID: O'Neil??? What's up with him the day? He's went all strange. Barry wait. Don't go. I'm sorry. I'm sorry.

BARRY: Do you really hate me?

DAVID: Naw. I never said I hated you anyroads.

CHRISSY: I did.

BARRY: I don't care about you.

DAVID: Chrissy doesn't mean it either.

BARRY: Prove it.

DAVID: How can I prove? Just accept the apology, jeezo.

BARRY: Prove it.

DAVID: Oh all right. Hey, I know, I'll tell you a secret.

CHRISSY: What? David don't tell him, he'll grass us up.

BARRY: How what've yous done?

CHRISSY: Nothing

BARRY: *(Very interested.)* What is it?

DAVID: You've got to promise not to tell anyone but.

BARRY: I'm not promising till I know what it is.

CHRISSY: See! David don't tell him.

DAVID: If I tell you, right, will you stay and then forget about us hating you?

CHRISSY: This is madness!

BARRY: Oh...all right, go.

DAVID: It was us.

BARRY: What was?

DAVID: Decky. It was us that made him run away.

BARRY: How? When?

DAVID: Last night. We were taking the mickey out of him for not being able to Bronco and he totally flaked and said he was off to the army. That's how he's no here.

BARRY: Ooooooooohhha, yous are totally dead.

DAVID: I know, I'm hating it.

CHRISSY: I never done nothing.

DAVID: You did so.

CHRISSY: No I never.

DAVID: Chrissy!!

BARRY: You're going to have to tell his dad.

DAVID: *(Nearly crying.)* How?

BARRY: 'Cause. Think about it. His mum and dad are really worried. If he's away to the army, he'll be on the Ayr road and the police'll find him. If something happens to him you'll never forget it.

CHRISSY: What's going to happen to him?

BARRY: Decky cannae even get on a swing without breaking a bone. God knows what'll happen to him on the Ayr road.

DAVID: Chrissy. I'm going over to Decky's house.

CHRISSY: *(Thinks about it for ages.)* I'll go with you, but I'm not saying anything about anything.

DAVID: I'll say it. Maybe we should tell my dad first?

BARRY: No! Just go, you won't get into trouble. I'll come too.

CHRISSY: David. Your mum's calling you in.

DAVID: *(Screaming at his mum.)* What???!!!

BARRY: She wants me. How do you think she wants to see me?

DAVID: I don't know. Do you want us to look after your bike?

BARRY: No way.

(BARRY exits pushing the bike.)

DAVID: Coming?

CHRISSY: Aye.

(CHRISSY exits gloomily. DAVID talks directly to the audience.)

DAVID: I remember what happened next very clearly. We walked along with Barry till we got to my bit. Barry padlocked his bike to the inside of our fence and went in. Me and Chrissy walked on to Decky's house, very, very, slowly. I had that fear in my belly that you only get now when your boss shouts at you for a mistake you know you made. I think it's called guilt. I used to get that feeling a lot when I was wee, but not as bad as this. We went in the back way to Decky's house, through the garden full of broken bogies and inflated inner tubes. I chapped the door. Chrissy wanted to just walk in, which is what he usually does, but I thought that the occasion required some manners. I was hating it and I would have ran away there and then had the door not opened. I'm a coward. I know that in my heart. I put on a good show, but I'm a coward in my heart. A woman I'd never seen before answered the door. I started crying. Chrissy stepped up and said 'it's our fault Decky's away to Ayr'. I looked up and saw the woman was crying too. She took my hand and led us into the hall. Then she just forgot about us and drifted into the kitchen. The house was jam-packed. There were people everywhere. But it was very quiet. Whispers and low rumbling conversations. We didn't know what to do, so we went to see if we could find his mum and dad. Chrissy went upstairs and I went into the living room. It was like I was invisible. No one looked at me or…no, that's not right. They looked at me for a split second and then they looked away. They could see something else. There was total silence in the living room, apart from Decky's dad. He was sitting forward in his chair with his head in his hands. His hands were huge and battered from years of working outside. The tears were streaming between his fingers as if his entire face was made from water.

(DAVID walks over to the swing, climbs on, workys up and Broncos. The lights go down.)

Sunday Afternoon.

(Lights up. DAVID sits on the swing. It's not moving. Adult BARRY enters. As with O'NEIL, he is still the same age as before and he acts like the young version, although he is not a child anymore. He doesn't speak for a while. He just sits on the swing next to DAVID.)

DAVID: What did my mum want?

BARRY: She wanted to tell me something to tell you.

DAVID: Why doesn't she just tell me?

BARRY: Just. I'm the oldest.

DAVID: Have you been crying?

BARRY: *(Nearly crying now.)* Na.

DAVID: Decky's dead isn't he?

BARRY: How d'you know?

DAVID: You should see it round his house. His dad's crying.

BARRY: Your mum's crying her eyes out. Your dad's back home. He says that when you're ready you've to go in.

DAVID: Ready for what? Do you know what happened?

BARRY: No, but they've caught the guy that done it?

DAVID: A guy done it? Killed him?

BARRY: Your mum says that the police might want to ask us stuff. She says we've to remember if we ever saw someone hanging around.

DAVID: What, up at the swings?

BARRY: Aye.

DAVID: But…is this where it happened? How could it be?

BARRY: How could it no?

DAVID: But we were with him all day yesterday up here. Right up to the end when he bombed it… He must have come back. I'll bet he came up here to…I'll bet he came up here to…practise, I'll bet he was learning to Bronco.

BARRY: No one knows.

DAVID: *I* know. I know. It was my fault after all.

BARRY: It wasn't your fault David. It was the guy's fault. The guy that done it. No one else has anything to do with it. It wasnae Decky, it wasnae me and it wasnae you. It was the guy.

DAVID: Do they know for sure that he was killed? He might have just fallen or something.

BARRY: I don't know. Your mum just said that they'd found the guy who'd done it so we werenae to get scared. She said Decky's in heaven.

DAVID: I wonder if it was sore when Decky was killed? If it was a guy why didn't he kill another guy instead of a wee kid like Decky? It's not fair. It's not fair. He was so wee.

BARRY: Your dad phoned my dad and he's coming down. I'll probably have to go back.

DAVID: I feel really weird. I kinda don't feel anything.

BARRY: I was crying then I stopped.

DAVID: I wonder if Chrissy knows?

BARRY: Where is he?

DAVID: He's over at Decky's house.

BARRY: He'll be hating it.

DAVID: What do we do now?

BARRY: I'll have to go to Ayr and get a black tie. Do you have
a black tie?

DAVID: No. My dad might.

BARRY: He'll be wearing it though.

DAVID: Oh…aye, I suppose he will. What do we do? I should
be crying or something.

BARRY: I'm waiting until I get back to Gran's before I cry. I
wonder if she knows? She never even met Decky though.
Think about it. Think about all the people who never met
him, who he would have met, the things he would have
done. He never even Broncoed a swing.

DAVID: Maybe he did. Maybe that was the last thing he did.
I hope he did. *(Gets up from the swing and talks directly
to the audience.)* Grief is a strange, strange thing. I went
through a nothing, no-man's land of emotions for weeks.
I was watching things from behind a two-way mirror. I
remember that colours seemed brighter. It was like getting
a new telly. The same programmes but a slightly sharper
picture. Then, *ages* after, I went hysterical. Just like that.
It wasn't that I was thinking about Decky or anything, I
just cracked up. Everyone would say 'he's been through
so much' and everything, but at the time I couldn't see
any connection. I didn't go to school for a while. I didn't
talk to anyone for about a month apart from my mum and
dad. Funny. Then, as the cliché dictates, time covered the
cracks. I would be doing something and a voice in my
head would say 'Hey, remember that Decky was killed'.
But the voice gets fainter and then just stops. In the few

days after I found the whole thing quite exciting. That sounds bad but it was so different. Everything changed. There were police, newspaper people, a TV crew and loads of people asking me stuff. It was a tiny coffin. It looked quite funny. Barry didn't come back for his holidays. We didn't speak for about eight years, until we met coincidentally in a pub in Glasgow. Chrissy went all hard. Bitter. He's a fighter by instinct. He was hard from then on in.

(Enter Adult CHRISSY. As with the others he still plays a nine-year-old. He is much harder now, though. He's covering everything up with a swagger.)

CHRISSY: What's up wi' yous?

DAVID: Have you not heard?

CHRISSY: About Decky? Aye. So.

DAVID: So??? What do you mean 'so'?

CHRISSY: Everyone's going nuts. You see his house. Everyone dies sometime. He was hanging about up at the swings all night, what did you expect?

DAVID: Shut up you.

CHRISSY: Look I know it's sad an' that but you'd be better just getting over it. It's not like you were his brother or anything. It's all right to cry and all of that if you're in his family but there's no point if you just hung about with him.

DAVID: Shut up! If we hadnae been saying all that stuff he wouldnae have come back and he'd still be here.

CHRISSY: And we'd still be taking the mickey out of him. Just 'cause he's – just 'cause he's no here people are going to be all 'Aw wee Decky was ace, man I was best pals with him' but they werenae. I'm no even going to the funeral.

DAVID: Aye ye are.

CHRISSY: No I'm no.

DAVID: You have to go!

CHRISSY: No I don't. I don't have to do nothing.

BARRY: It's all right, he can do what he wants.

DAVID: Eh?

BARRY: He can. Who told you Chrissy?

CHRISSY: I was coming down the stairs and I heard two women talking about it in the hall.

BARRY: *(Tentatively.)* What were they saying?

CHRISSY: What do you think? And they were just as bad. They were loving it. They were pretending to be sad, but you could tell that they were enjoying it. Probably the most interesting thing that's happened to them in their whole lives. They never even knew Decky but they're straight round his house greetin'. I hate people. Well I'm not doing it. I'm not joining in on it 'cause it's not real.

BARRY: What were they saying?

CHRISSY: Ach, who cares. It's not true anyway, probably. They said he was found in the Bank Burn.

DAVID: *(Horrified.)* No way.

CHRISSY: They said the guy had pulled his pants down.

(DAVID lets out a wee laugh. He knows it's wrong but he couldn't help it. There's a silence. They half understand.)

DAVID: You have to go to the funeral man. You have to.

CHRISSY: How? Who's gonna make me? Eh? *(To DAVID.)* You? *(To BARRY.)* You? *(To DAVID again and now just barely stopping the tears but not moving an inch.)* I'll fight ye if you want. I'll fight ye I mean it. I don't care! I'LL FIGHT YE!!

(Adult O'NEIL enters. DAVID looks to him for help. CHRISSY follows his gaze and turns on O'NEIL who is scared and hesitant.)

CHRISSY: What do you want?

O'NEIL: I wanted a go on my swing before I go.

BARRY: Go? Where are you going?

O'NEIL: Me and my mum are going to England for a wee while. We're staying with my Aunty Jean.

DAVID: You can't go now! Don't you know what's happened?

O'NEIL: *(Sadly and shyly.)* I just wanted one last go on the swings. I just wanted to Bronco again to see if I could still do it.

CHRISSY: No one's going on these swings.

BARRY: What?

CHRISSY: I said no one's going on these swings! These swings are finished. No one's going to Bronco ever again on these swings.

O'NEIL: I need to.

DAVID: You cannae stop every single person that comes up here wanting to go on the swings. They're not your swings.

CHRISSY: Just watch me.

(CHRISSY smashes up the swings.)

CHRISSY: I've killed them. See? It's as easy as that. Let's see you Bronco them now.

O'NEIL: It wasnae me.

CHRISSY: So?

O'NEIL: How come everyone forgets that I'm nine as well as all yous? Everyone thinks I'm old. But I'm not. I'm nine. It's not fair.

CHRISSY: So?

O'NEIL: I don't know when I'll be back. I'll see you.

DAVID: See you O'Neil.

BARRY: But I'll be away when you get back.

O'NEIL: I'll see yous.

(O'NEIL takes a last sad look at the swings before he exits.)

DAVID: *(To CHRISSY.)* I'm sorry.

CHRISSY: Look, just leave us alone right. I don't care about stupid swings. I don't care... Don't come round for me either, 'cause I WON'T COME OUT!!

(CHRISSY runs off stage.)

BARRY: I'll bet your mum wants us in the house.

DAVID: I'll bet.

BARRY: You coming down?

DAVID: Aye.

BARRY: It's terrible isn't it? I wish God was real.

DAVID: So do I. Why do you think the guy...?

BARRY: What?

DAVID: I don't know. I want my mum.

BARRY: I want my mum too. I feel wee. Let's go.

(Exit BARRY who touches the swings as he goes.)

DAVID: You know when you watch the news and you see the daily child abduction story; the smiling school photo in the corner of the screen and the stern-faced newsreader, unable to believe that they are saying yet again the phrase 'was last seen alive'; do you know when you see that, you always say 'I can't imagine what the parents are going through', do you feel that you're telling a lie? I do. Because when I close my eyes for that split second during the teatime news, when I close my eyes and say 'not again', I know *exactly* what the parents are going through. Because the truth is that not only can we imagine what the parents are going through, we can imagine what the child went through. And if we can imagine that... But we don't. We can't limit imagination, but we can censor it. Shut it out and pretend it's mute. We can push that down and down and down so that it only seeps out for seconds at a time. How could we live if we didn't? How could we sleep? We live in a world that's not easily woken up. We're so used to shoving that part of our imagination down that most new atrocities just get plunged into the cellar. Child abuse? Heard it, terrible but down you go. Rape? That old chestnut, down, down, down. It's human. We have to let these things drift away in our mind because if we had them upfront all the time we'd kill ourselves. Like this. This story. Could we push this down? That a man took wee Decky from the swings and thrust him violently up against the glass and let him look at the worst part of adulthood, and then killed him? Can we go on after that? Yes. Yes, we can, we did. It took a while and like Decky on the swings, we still hold on with one hand, but we jump all the same. I've made it into this story to help me. Somedays I never even think about it. Wee Decky...

(Enter DECKY who happily runs on stage and untangles one of the swings from where CHRISSY put it and begins to worky up.)

DAVID: I've worked it out now. I have a system for living. You see when the news comes on and I close my eyes, I have a picture in my mind. It's the most beautiful, free, childlike, fun, important thing in the world. Because it's there, in that blink, in that instant...that Decky does a Bronco.

(And so he does. The swing swoops over the bar and he is launched into the air. The lights snap off while he's still flying.)

The End.

WWW.OBERONBOOKS.COM

Follow us on www.twitter.com/@oberonbooks
& www.facebook.com/OberonBooksLondon

Printed in the USA
CPSIA information can be obtained
at www.ICGtesting.com
LVHW021003171024
794056LV00004B/1301

9 781840 022438